UN Peace Operations

Part II

Hostage Taking of Peacekeepers

UN Peace Operations

Part II

Hostage Taking of Peacekeepers

Edited by

A K Bardalai and Pradeep Goswami

A Joint USI - ICWA Publication

Vij Books India Pvt Ltd
New Delhi (India)

Published by

Vij Books India Pvt Ltd
(Publishers, Distributors & Importers)
2/19, Ansari Road
Delhi – 110 002
Phones: 91-11-43596460, 91-11-47340674
Mob: 98110 94883
e-mail: contact@vijpublishing.com
web : www.vijbooks.in

First Published in India in 2021

ISBN: 978-93-90917-22-8

Contents

Preface

India's deepening engagement with the United Nations (UN) is based on its steadfast commitment to multilateralism and dialogue as the key for achieving shared goals and addressing common challenges faced by the global community. These include those related to peace building and peacekeeping, sustainable development, poverty eradication, environment, climate change, terrorism, disarmament, human rights, health and pandemics, migration, cyber security, space and frontier technologies like Artificial Intelligence, comprehensive reform of the United Nations, including the reform of the Security Council, among others.

India was among the select members of the UN that signed the Declaration by United Nations at Washington on 01 January 1942. India also participated in the historic UN Conference of International Organisation at San Francisco from 25 April to 26 June 1945. India strongly supports the purposes and principles of the UN, and has made significant contributions to implementing the goals of the Charter, and the evolution of the UN's specialised programmes and agencies. India believes that the UN and the norms of international relations that it has fostered remain the most efficacious means for tackling today's global challenges. India is steadfast in its efforts to work with the comity of nations, in the spirit of multilateralism, to achieve comprehensive and equitable solutions to all problems facing us including development and poverty eradication, climate change etc.

India has a long and distinguished history of service in UN peacekeeping, having contributed more personnel than any other country. To date, more than 253,000 Indians have served in 49 of the 71 UN peacekeeping missions established around the world since 1948. Currently, around 5,500 troops & police personnel from India are deployed in eight of 13 UN peacekeeping missions, the fifth-highest amongst troop-contributing countries.

Commencing with its participation in the UN operation in Korea in the 1950s, India's mediatory role in resolving the stalemate over prisoners of war in Korea led to the signing of the armistice ending the Korean War. India chaired the five-member Neutral Nations Repatriation Commission while the Indian Custodian Force supervised the process of interviews and repatriation that followed. The UN entrusted Indian armed forces with subsequent peace missions in the Middle East, Cyprus, and the Congo (since 1971, Zaire). India also served as chair of the three international commissions for supervision and control for Vietnam, Cambodia, and Laos established by the 1954 Geneva Accords on Indochina.

India has a long tradition of sending women on UN peacekeeping missions. In 2007, India became the first country to deploy an all-women contingent to a UN peacekeeping mission. Medical care, veterinary support to the domestic animals of the local population and constructional activities are among the many services Indian peacekeepers provide to the communities in which they serve on behalf of the organisation.

India has provided a number of senior level mission leaders including Head of the Mission, Force Commanders, Deputy Head of the Mission, Deputy Force Commanders and senior staff officers to various missions. Besides the Force Commanders, India also had the honour of providing two Military Advisors, one woman Police Adviser and two Deputy Military Advisors to the Secretary-General of the UN. The first Indian all women contingent in peacekeeping mission, a Formed Police Unit, was deployed in 2007 to the UN Operation in Liberia (UNMIL). India was the first country to contribute to the Trust Fund on Sexual Exploitation and Abuse, which was set up in 2016. India's longstanding service has not come without cost, hundreds of Indian peacekeepers have paid the ultimate price while serving with the UN. India has lost more peacekeepers than any other member state.

In the more than seven decades of UN peacekeeping operations' interventions in different kinds of conflict, peacekeepers always faced multiple challenges when it comes to implementing the mandate. As time passes, these challenges have become more complex, undermining the ability of the peace operations to deliver in the conflict zone. This is also what the Department of UN Peace Operation's survey of August 2019 indicates. Besides the inherent lag between the intent and the outcome in all spheres of the activities, there could be several other strategic and operational reasons for slow progress of reform in the field. This is not to conclude that so far no reform has taken place. India has been one of the oldest contributors in peacekeeping operations and, hence, is a vast repository of the best practices.

The United Service Institution (USI) of India in past has taken the lead in providing the platform for organising discourse and research in the field of UN peace operations to put across an Indian perspective on a few most crucial attributes of the current challenges that face reform of the UN peace operations. At this juncture, USI of India (https://usiofindia.org), the oldest think tank in India, in collaboration with Indian Council of World Affairs (ICWA) (https://www.icwa.in), the premium think tank of India's Ministry of External Affairs, Government of India, planned to conduct a series of webinars on UN peace operations in 2021 on the following themes:

> Theme 1 - India and UN Peace Operations: Principles of UN Peacekeeping and Mandate.

> Theme 2 - UN Peace Operations: Hostage-taking of Peacekeepers.

> Theme 3 - Effectiveness of UN Peace Operations.

> Theme 4 - Protection of civilians in complex UN Peace Operations.

> Theme 5 - Peace and Security: the Role of women.

> Theme 6 - Interoperability Challenges in multidimensional peace operations: Role of senior mission leaders (Head of the Mission and Force Commanders).

> Theme 7 - Peacekeeping Reform: An Indian perspective.

Inaugural UN webinar was conducted on 27 Feb 2021 on 'India and UN Peace Operations: Principles of UN Peacekeeping and Mandate'. A good comprehension of the meaning of the principles of peacekeeping is important because the way these are interpreted will continue to impact the performance of peace operations. Therefore, this should be the topic of discussion and debate as part of the pre-deployment training in the troop-contributing countries and post-deployment training in the mission area. This would help to reduce the scope of misinterpretation of the nuances of principles of peacekeeping and its impact on the effectiveness of the mission. Accordingly, the first webinar was held with the following sub-themes:

> Principles of UN Peacekeeping, its continued relevance and mandate implementation.

> Relevance of the principle of 'Use of Force' in United Nations Stabilization Mission in Congo (MONUSCO) and United Nations Mission in South Sudan (UNMISS).

> Contribution of traditional peace operations [United Nations Interim Force in Lebanon (UNIFIL) and United Nations Disengagement Force (UNDOF)] for sustainable peace.

The second webinar was conducted on 29 Jun 2021 on 'UN Peace Operations: Hostage-taking of Peacekeepers'. Hostage-taking is not a new phenomenon. Even the ancient Romans took hostages of princes as a guarantee to the obligations made for their conquered regions. In medieval times, knights used to be taken hostage for ransom. Some would, however, like to use the word kidnap in place of a hostage. Whether hostage-taking or kidnapping, these are all part of extortionist terrorist acts and there is always a motive. This practice has flourished in contemporary times with the criminal gangs either for ransom or for forcing the hands of the authority to allow them to escape unharmed.

There are many complications in handling a hostage crisis. There are advocates of the hard-line approach who believe that succumbing to the pressure and releasing terrorists will allow the terrorists to terrorise the authority again. Therefore, no matter if the hostages cannot be rescued, for the sake of the nation, no compromise should be made. On the other hand, those who support a flexible approach believe in pragmatism and want to combine deterrence with negotiation. It effectively means that in absence of a workable military option, to accept the demand of the terrorist in exchange for the release of the hostages. No matter which option is exercised, there will be a cost to pay. Neither of these options is an easy one.

Why take peacekeepers hostage? Peacekeepers are supposed to be the enablers and get deployed in the conflict zone to help bring peace and save human lives. So, what happens when the enablers themselves become the victim of the extortionist act of the terrorists? Peacekeepers will be denied their freedom and will not be able to deliver in implementing the mandate and, thereby, would impact the effectiveness of the mission. Following a hard-line approach invariably invite retaliation. This possibly is what worked in the minds of the senior mission leaders of UNPROFOR when between 05 and 11 July 1995, the Serbs took 30 peacekeeper hostages, and the mission leaders refused the get NATO airstrike. One of the theories for not getting the airstrike is that airstrike against the Serbs would further antagonise them, who would retaliate against the UN peacekeepers in different locations. The demand of the Serbs prevailed, the Dutch peacekeepers had to surrender and, eventually, thousands of innocent Bosnian Muslims were killed. Hostage-taking need not be always like kidnapping. It can be also in the form of house arrest. During the peak of the civil war in Angola after Jonas Savimbi of UNITA lost his election in 1991, the UNITA rebels returned to the jungle and picked up their arms again. Side by side, the rebels held a few unarmed military observers under house arrest. The observers were denied freedom of movement and could not report on activity by the rebels. The use of military force to lift the seize was not an option since it was an observer mission. It did take some good negotiating skills to lift the seize. The rebels, however, did not demand anything. It was because their action was simply displaying their anger against the international community alleging that the election was rigged.

Response to a hostage crisis will depend on several variables which will have to be considered in the hostage rescue strategy. This webinar discussed two different situations necessitating two different approaches with the following sub-themes:

> Overview of the hostage crisis, its implications and tenets of rescue strategy.

> Emerging trends in hostage-taking of peacekeepers.

> Strategy & challenges of hostage rescue when peacekeepers from larger TCCs are taken hostage (UNAMSIL).

> Strategy & challenges when peacekeepers from smaller TCCs are taken hostage (UNDOF).

This monograph is a compilation of talks by eminent speakers during the second webinar, 'UN Peace Operations: Hostage-taking of Peacekeepers'.

About the Participants

Major General BK Sharma, AVSM, SM (Retd)** is the Director of the USI of India, India's oldest think tank established by the British in 1870. He has tenanted prestigious assignments in India including command of a mountain division on the China border and Senior Faculty Member at the National Defence College, New Delhi. He has represented his country at the UN as Military Observer in Central America and has been India's Defence Attaché in Central Asia. He specialises in Strategic Net Assessment methodology, Scenario Building and Strategic Gaming.

Dr TCA Raghavan, a former officer of the Indian Foreign Service, was the Indian High Commissioner to Pakistan (2013-15) and currently is the Director-General of ICWA. He had earlier served as Deputy High Commissioner in Pakistan (2003-2007) and High Commissioner to Singapore from 2009 to 2013. He has also served in Kuwait, the United Kingdom, and Bhutan. His first book was published in January 2020: "Attendant Lords, Bairam Khan and Abdur Rahim - Courtiers and Poets in Mughal India". His latest book was published recently and is entitled "The People Next Door - The curious history of India's relations with Pakistan".

Major General PK Goswami, VSM (Retd) is the Deputy Director at the USI of India and chief coordinator for series of USI – ICWA webinars on UN peace operations. He was Military Observer with United Nations Verification Mission at Angola (UNAVEM) in 1991-92 and Senior Faculty at National Defence College, New Delhi. He represented

National Defence College, India at the 16th ASEAN Regional Forum for Heads of Defence Universities, Colleges and Institutions in Beijing, China in Nov 2012.

Shri Dinkar Srivastava, IFS retired as Indian Ambassador to Iran in 2015 and during this tenure he negotiated the MOU for Indian participation in Chabahar Port. In his earlier appointments in MEA in UN Political Division, he dealt with Indian participation in UN Peacekeeping Operations in Cambodia, Somalia, Rwanda, Angola, Mozambique, Sierra Leone and Lebanon. He negotiated the release of UN peacekeepers taken as hostage in Sierra Leone in 2000. He also dealt with J&K issues in the UN fora as well as the diplomatic fall-out of Pokhran II nuclear tests. Presently, he is Independent Director, India Ports Global Ltd (IPGL) for the development of Chabahar Port, Distinguished Fellow in Vivekananda International Foundation and Distinguished Professor, Symbiosis International University.

Colonel (Dr) KK Sharma (Retd) was a military observer in UNTAC, Cambodia in 1992 - 1993. He was an active member in planning and writing of UN Capstone Doctrine on peacekeeping and manuals for trainers in the Office of High Commissioner of Human Rights, Geneva. He has been associated with the planning cell of peacekeeping operations in Army HQ and was a founding member of starting Centre for UN Peacekeeping under the USI of India. He is PhD in Management from Zurich, Switzerland, and presently a Professor and Dean, Global Education Programs in Chitkara University, responsible to mentor and administer UG courses in academic collaboration with the University of Windsor and Trent University, Canada.

Lieutenant General Vijay Kumar Jetley, PVSM, UYSM (Retd) is a veteran of the Indian Army and has held several important military command and staff appointments; and superannuated in December 2004 as the Master General of Ordnance. He had served as Sector Commander and Senior Plans Officer of the United Nations Iran Iraq Military Observer Group (UNIIMOG) and subsequently as first Force Commander of the United Nations Mission in Sierra Leone (UNAMSIL). Once rebels abrogated the existing peace treaty, attacked UN peacekeepers and captured a few hundred of them; as Force Commander, he conducted series of multi-national military operations, including the world-famous Operation Khukri.

Lieutenant General IS Singha, AVSM, VSM (Retd) is a veteran of the Indian Army and has held several important military command and staff appointments at various levels both in India and abroad. He was the Chief Logistics Officer in the United Nations Mission in Ethiopia and Eretria and subsequently the Force Commander and Head of Mission of the United Nations Disengagement Observer Force at Golan Heights (UNDOF). After retirement, General is presently the Director of Global and Government Affairs at TAC Security, a leading global cybersecurity company that is working in partnership with USI of India.

Major General (Dr) AK Bardalai (Retd) is a veteran of the Indian Army and has held various command and staff assignments at different levels, including the command of an infantry division. He was also the Commandant of the Indian Military Training Team in Bhutan from October 2011 to January 2014. He was a Military Observer in the United Nations Verification Mission in Angola in 1991-92 and Deputy Head of the Mission and Deputy Force Commander of United Nations Interim Force in Lebanon (UNIFIL) from 2008 to 2010. He is the recipient of PhD for his research on UN Peace Operations from Tilburg University (the Netherlands).

Concept Note

UN Peace Keeping Operations: Hostage-taking of UN Peacekeepers

Earlier, UN peacekeeping was generally associated with traditional peace operations inter-state conflicts. Peacekeepers were deployed inside a neutral and mutually agreed zone with the expectation of supervising an agreed ceasefire and prevent the recurrence of the violation until the cessation of hostilities. Since the armies of the states who were at war were separated by the peacekeepers deployed in the temporary security zone, they generally did not encounter the civilian population or the military of the states except in peculiar situations like deployment of UNIFIL in Lebanon. However, with the increasing number of intra-state conflicts and the growing intensity of the violence, the peacekeepers often themselves become the target of violence. The threat to the life of peacekeepers can come in varying forms like getting caught in the crossfire of intra-armed group rivalry, direct attack by the armed elements or even at times being taken as hostages. Hostage-taking of the peacekeepers by the armed groups in the conflict zone is often politically motivated. To counter the growing physical threat to the peacekeepers, there is now more emphasis on force protection measures and robust rules of engagement. Even the mandates have become stronger, allowing the peacekeepers to use force and any other means as necessary to ensure their safety. But to free the hostages from their captors has multiple challenges. The use of force is generally retaliated and in the case of missions, where only unarmed observers are deployed, it will need a different approach to secure the release of hostages. The challenges can be more complicated when there is a presence of armed terrorist groups in the conflict zone. Eventually, response strategy to hostage-taking cannot be uniform and would vary as per the prevailing crisis. Analysis of the past hostage-taking incidents, however, is important to draw lessons for the prevention and resolution of such crises in future. This webinar will deliberate on the nuances of challenges of hostage and response from the UN and the TCCs. The webinar seeks to address the following issues:

1. An overview of the threat of hostage-taking of peacekeepers, implications, and tenets of macro rescue strategy.

2. Strategies, planning and execution of a hostage rescue in the context of two field missions (traditional and non-traditional peacekeeping operations):

    (a) Strategy and challenges of hostage rescue when peacekeepers from larger TCCA are taken hostages (UNAMSIL).

    (b) Strategy when peacekeepers from smaller TCCs are taken hostages (UNDOF).

Opening Remarks

Dr TCA Raghavan

I am delighted that we are now beginning the second webinar on the ICWA - USI joint platform on peacekeeping. In this project of a series of planned webinars, our two institutions aim to create synergies between ourselves by studying and discussing in-depth India's interface with the UN by focusing in particular on Peacekeeping. It is also our view that the respective audiences of ICWA and USI events will benefit from this synergy and thereby make for more.

In the past, UN peacekeeping was generally associated with traditional peace operations in an environment of inter-state conflicts. Peacekeepers held a mutually agreed neutral zone to supervise an agreed ceasefire and prevent the occurrence and recurrence of violations to it until the final cessation of hostilities. In such a scenario, they generally did not encounter the civilian population except in peculiar situations like the deployment of UNIFIL in Lebanon. Today, however, peacekeepers often operate in volatile environments and with the specific mandate to protect civilians. Likewise, alongside peacekeeping operations, special political missions have increasingly complex mandates and are being deployed into ever more dangerous situations.

With the increasing number of intra-state conflicts and growing intensity of violence in the UN mission areas, peacekeepers themselves often become the target. The threat to peacekeepers is varying like getting caught up in a crossfire of intra-armed group rivalry, direct attack or even at times being taken as hostages. Hostage-taking of peacekeepers is often politically motivated to try and negotiate from a position of strength. But a hostage incident usually impacts the ability of a mission to deliver on its mandate and required humanitarian assistance, since all associated activities are often suspended until the incident is resolved.

Thus, ensuring the safety and security of peacekeepers is vital for fulfilling the organisation's responsibilities and it also strategically impacts the efficacy of mandate execution, force generation, the evolution of peace operations, and sustaining the relevance of the UN in the maintenance of international peace and security.

The UN's concern about malicious and violent attacks on its peacekeepers has been reflected in the HIPPO (High-Level Independent Panel on UN Peace Organizations) Report, 2015. The report states that there is a "…widening gap between what is being asked of UN peace operations today and what they can deliver. This gap can be – must be – narrowed to ensure that the Organization's peace operations can respond effectively and appropriately to the challenges to come…". While UN peace operations have become more professional and capable over the past decade, the HIPPO report highlights the prevalence of significant chronic challenges such as resources for prevention and mediation being scarce and the UN often being too slow to engage with emerging crises. The report also highlighted how too often, "…mandate and missions are produced based on templates instead of tailored to support situation-specific political strategies and technical and military approaches come at the expense of strengthened political efforts …".

To counter this growing threat to the peacekeepers, there is, therefore, now more emphasis on force protection measures and robust rules of engagement. Even peacekeeping mandates have become stronger allowing peacekeepers to use force and any other means as necessary to ensure their safety. But to free hostages from the captors has multiple challenges. The use of force is generally retaliated and in the case of missions where only unarmed observers are deployed, it will need a different approach to secure the release of hostages. Challenges can be even more complicated when there is a presence of armed terrorist groups in the conflict zone. Eventually, response strategy to hostage-taking cannot be uniform and would vary as per the prevailing crisis. While many of the relevant safety and security issues have been identified, they have not often been highlighted holistically and addressed with sufficient priority.

Thus, analysis of the past hostage-taking incidents is important to draw lessons for the prevention and resolution of such crises in future.

I am grateful to all the distinguished participants who have joined in today. Their wealth of experience and knowledge will allow us to delve into both the tactical as also the larger strategic realm of policy-related issues and further understand the interplay in these two dimensions of the current predicaments of peacekeeping.

Overview of the Hostage Crisis, its Implications and tenets of Rescue Strategy

Shri Dinkar Srivastava, IFS (Retd)
(Moderator)

Introduction

The UN Charter does not mention peacekeeping but the concept evolved with time. It has since become the most visible aspect of activities of the world body. The cold war years saw some major peacekeeping operations in Sinai, Congo, and Syria. However, the progress was slow due to the deadlock in the Security Council. The end of the cold war removed this blockage and there was an expansion of the UN's activities. As a result, the first forty-five years of the UN had seen the adoption of 687 resolutions by the Security Council. In the next decade, this number nearly doubled to 1334.

The expansion of the UN's activities in the 1990s was accompanied by a change in the nature of peacekeeping. Consequently, as the focus of UN peacekeeping shifted from inter-state to intra-state conflicts, it brought in a new set of problems. But the change from inter-state to intra-state conflicts is part of the larger problem of UN peacekeeping and goes beyond the issue of hostage-taking.

The hostage situations of UNDOF and UNAMSIL should be seen in the context of the time, the structure of the mission and the mandates. UNDOF is a traditional Observer Mission to observe a truce between two states – Israel and Syria. On the other hand, UNAMSIL has established a generation later in 1999. Its mandate was to deal with an internal situation. In Sierra Leone, 500 troops and observers of 13 different countries were taken hostage in May 2000. India had provided the largest contingent and, hence, was given the role of Force Commander. The responsibility of resolving the hostage crisis hence devolved on India.

However, in the case of UNDOF, 180 observers were held hostage in different incidents over two years between 2012-14. UNDOF was established in 1974 with a mandate to supervise the separation zone between Syria and Israel. In 2013, taking advantage of Syria's internal problem, a few non-state actors took a few peacekeepers hostage. Taking hostage from UNDOF could be because of several reasons ranging from seeking publicity, looking for affiliation to ISIS and Al Nusra, getting funding and ransom to restricting the freedom of movement of the UN peacekeepers.

Strategy for Hostage Rescue

There cannot be a single strategy for hostage rescue because the events leading to a hostage situation and the factors influencing the crisis will vary from conflict to conflict. Besides, being an inter-governmental body, the UN does not deal with non-state actors in normal circumstances. There are, however, a few questions that are common in all hostage situations. These are:

> ➤ Whom to negotiate with? Rebel groups are often amorphous groups without necessarily a unified command and control.

> ➤ Rebel groups are usually not recognised by the UN. This adds to the problem of dealing with them. UN cannot lend them legitimacy.

> ➤ What interest do the rebel groups have in negotiation if they have no stake in the peace- process.

> ➤ Do jihadi groups have any interest in negotiation? Or they are only interested in making a statement?

The strategy to rescue hostages hence should take into consideration the above questions. There is yet another bigger question as to *why* both hostage situations arose? A mismatch between the mandate and the resources resulting in thin deployment of troops on the ground could be one of the reasons for non-state actors being able to take hostage. The UN peace operations are sometimes underpinned by peace agreements, which if and when break down, because of any reason, lead to a situation with additional burden on the operation. This is what happened in the case of UNAMSIL. In the case of UNDOF, the peace agreement between Syria and Israel was holding. But the outbreak of civil war in Syria had introduced new actors who had an interest in challenging the status quo.

UNAMSIL

UNAMSIL was established following the Lome Peace agreement of July 1999. The mandate of the UNSC resolution 1270 of October 1999 envisaged essentially a support role for the UNAMSIL while the regional peacekeeping force the Economic Community Military Observer Group (ECOMOG) was to continue to provide security, conduct operations, and ensure the implementation of the peace agreement. But Nigeria, which had provided the bulk of troops for ECOMOG, pulling out of the operation in early 2000 upset the balance of the troops' deployment. It was because ECOMOG was a larger force with around 15,000 troops while UNAMSIL had 6,000 troops. The situation further got complicated when the peace accord between the Sierra Leone government and the rebel group – Revolutionary United Front (RUF) broke down. These two developments had fundamentally altered the context in which UNAMSIL was deployed.

UNAMSIL's mandate has two major flaws. *One,* there was a complete mismatch between the mandate and the resources provided. The UNSCR 1270 mandated UNAMSIL with a force of 6,000 troops to conduct operations in conjunction with ECOMOG which was a much larger force. *Two,* after Nigeria pulled out of ECOMOG, UNAMSIL's mandate was revised under UNSCR 1289 of February 2000 with an enhanced force level of 11,000 troops, which, however, was below the previous force level when it operated along with ECOMOG. That apart, when the trouble broke out in May 2000, UNAMSIL was yet to reach even the sanctioned strength of 11,000.

The under-resourced operation had to struggle with an overly ambitious mandate. UNAMSIL had to discharge all the previous tasks including disarmament, originally assigned to ECOMOG. In addition, UNSCR 1289 gave additional tasks to UNAMSIL. This included facilitating 'free flow of people, goods and humanitarian assistance along specified thoroughfares'. This resulted in the deployment of the limited force over an extended area, including a few remote locations. This was one of the major reasons for which the contingents at Koidu and Kailahun were surrounded by the rebels.

Hostage Crisis

The RUF took 500 UN peacekeepers as hostages. While nearly half of these were released, the hostage situation continued in two areas. A small group of 23 troops was taken hostage at

Kuiva. A larger group of around 250 troops were surrounded in Kailahun. This included 220 Indians apart from around 10 military observers from other countries. The larger group at Kailahun, who were armed, could have attempted a break-out. But this would have endangered the lives of the smaller group which was completely disarmed. Their release could only be effected through negotiations.

The problem was with whom to negotiate? After the arrest of RUF leader Foday Sankoh, the rebel chain of command had broken down. The UN or the Indian government had no contact with the rebels. It was decided to send a delegation of the Government of India consisting of Lt Gen NC Vij, the Director-General of Military Operations of the army (later COAS), Shri BS Lali, Joint Secretary of MoD and Shri Dinkar Srivastava, Joint Secretary (UNP), MEA to Sierra Leone. The delegation was also to proceed to New York, Washington, and London to explore bilateral contacts.

Negotiation and Rescue Operation

On arrival in Sierra Leone, the delegation had an initial meeting with Mr Oluyemi Adeniji, the Special Representative of the Secretary-General to UNAMSIL. On his advice, it was decided to establish contact with Charles Taylor, President of Liberia. While the rest of the delegation went on to New York, Washington, and London, Shri Dinkar Srivastava stayed back in Sierra Leone for negotiations with the rebels. The Indian High Commissioner to Ghana was also sent to Liberia for approaching Charles Taylor bilaterally. Charles Taylor deputed Ms D Musuleng Cooper, the former Foreign Minister of Liberia to visit Sierra Leone to 'facilitate' the talks. The negotiations took place in Free Town; Charles Taylor obviously did not want to give the impression that his government was involved. Ms Cooper, who introduced herself to me as Big Mama, had the most delicate task. She had to help the Indian delegation without admitting any link of her country with the rebel group that it was backing.

It was only after the group of 23 soldiers was released at Kuiva on 29 June that it was possible to launch a military operation by UNAMSIL 'Operation Khukhri' for lifting the siege on the larger group of 221 troops and 11 military observers at Kailahun. Some of the western media had highlighted UK's role in lifting the siege. These reports are highly exaggerated. The UK had just one frigate offshore and some troops in Free Town airport. The operation was conducted by UNAMSIL with Indian troops in the lead, who bore all the risks in the operation which was inland, deep in the jungle, close to the Liberian border.

UNDOF

The hostage situation on Golan Heights was slightly different. As mentioned earlier, there was no breakdown of the peace accord. It was the consequent effect of the worsening situation in Syria after the Arab Spring of 2011. UNDOF was an Observer Mission. Its mandate and location had nothing to do with the internal problem of Syria. However, as the civil war escalated, non-state actors multiplied. By 2014, the rise of ISIS had increased the danger manifold leading to danger to the peacekeepers and a series of separate hostage-taking events. Eventually, the hostages were released unharmed after prolonged negotiation by the Head of the Mission and the Force Commander of UNDOF and also the UN.

Conclusion

Strategy for hostage rescue must consider several crucial factors. A realistic analysis of the threat, the prevailing geopolitical situation, status, or influence of the troop-contributing countries whose peacekeepers have been taken hostage, military capability of the peacekeeping mission to respond are a few such important factors. Consequently, the strategy for hostage rescue will vary from conflict to conflict. In Sierra Leone, it was the combination of negotiations and the use of force. In Golan Heights, it was simply by negotiation.

In Sierra Leone, it was possible to take peacekeepers hostage because the mission lacked adequate resources. Though the UNSC had sanctioned 11,000 troops when the trouble broke out, the boots on the ground were only 6,000. The deployment of UN peacekeepers over an extended area in small strength made it easier for the rebels to surround them and take hostage. In situations where the break-down of the peace accord forces the peacekeeping mission to shift from peacekeeping to peace-enforcement, the mission needs a stepped-up force level. The release of 23 unarmed peacekeepers at Kuiva was the essential pre-condition for the launch of Operation Khukhri. Skilful negotiation by Shri Dinkar Srivastava, Joint Secretary (UNP) with Ms D. Musuleng Cooper, President Charles Taylor's special envoy, made the release possible. On the other hand, the credit for the success of Operation Khukhri goes to the Indian troops under the command of General Jetley. Contrary to some of the media reports, the British played little or no role in it.

UNDOF, on the other hand, did not have the luxury to use force like UNAMSIL. The hostages were from a smaller TCC that lacked the requisite military muscle to respond with force. Even the mission as a whole did not have the resources to mount a military operation.

In a war-like situation that was in Syria, the position of lightly armed UN Observers is extremely precarious. While the member states are bound by UNSC resolutions and the Geneva Conventions, non-state actors show scant regard to either.

UN Peacekeepers as Hostages: Causes, Existing Framework & UN Strategy

Colonel (Dr) KK Sharma (Retd)

"Nobody attacks a stronger opponent"

Introduction

Peacekeeping (PK) is a risky activity and a certain number of casualties may occur even if all the necessary preventive measures are taken. If it was not full of risk, the UN will not deploy armed blue-helmeted contingents. A look at the UN Department of Peace Operations (UN DPO) webpage shows 4077 fatalities of peacekeepers since 1948 till 31 March 2021 (UN DPO, 2021). Amongst the high casualty PK missions were those in Congo, Lebanon, and Darfur. The UN has seen peaks of hostility related fatalities in the 1960s, 90s and in the period 2013 to 2019. But when viewed from a hostage-taking point of view, one finds very few fatalities compared to the actual figures – divided by the UN into accidents, illnesses and malicious acts. Based on the increasing trends of ever rising casualties in 2013, a high-level committee was appointed which gave a scathing report on the functioning of PK operations at all levels. The report underlined that the UN and troop contributing/police contributing countries (TCCs/PCCs) needed to adapt to a new reality: the blue helmet and the United Nations flag no longer offer 'natural'

13

protection (UN DPO, 2017). SIPRI had studied the trends in fatalities due to malicious acts against the peacekeepers and a policy brief by Van Der Lijn and Smit (2015) stated that data on deaths among UN peacekeepers between 1990 and 2015 indicated that fatalities have not become more frequent in absolute or relative terms. The study showed that the rate of fatalities among uniformed personnel in UN PK operations has steadily decreased, in relative terms, since the early 1990s. The number of fatalities due to malicious acts appeared high but only when Mali PK operations are factored in.

As is well documented, the post-cold war period saw most intra-state complex operations; and consequently, the PK environment changed dramatically. It witnessed larger deployments of armed peacekeepers, with a growing intensity of the violence against them. Hostage-taking by the armed groups for their political motives is one such UN defined malicious act. However, violence against the peacekeepers was there even before 1989 though sporadic and limited in scale. UN mission in Congo of 1960s witnessed armed clashes, attacks and tactical battles around Katanga province. India lost 39 soldiers, a part of 174 lives lost so far by the country. But there were very few incidents of hostage like situations and contingents in Congo and Gaza were adequately equipped for the scale of expected violence. Till 31 May 2021, there have been 1073 peacekeeper deaths 'due to malicious acts' (UN DPO, 2021). The first peak was around 1960-62 and included deployments in Suez and Congo. The second in 1992-96 included UN missions in Rwanda, Somalia, Cambodia, and former Yugoslavia. The third began in 2011, 'became critical in 2013' and continued into 2017 (UN DPO, 2017).

An interesting point of the overall conflict and UN peace operations comes from a study on the global armed conflicts by Licklider (1995). The study stated that 58 out of a total of 93 civil conflicts till the end of cold war were finally settled in some form or other, while the remainder continued. Out of these, only 24% (14) were solved by negotiations and remaining (76%) ended with the military victories. Additionally, fighting resumed in seven of the 14 conflicts which were initially ended by negotiation. The overall success rate of negotiated settlements, therefore, was around 12% out of the internal wars that ended.

The purpose of this paper is to analyse main causes and implications in a peacekeepers' hostage-taking situation and possible policy frameworks and UN strategy for a peaceful resolution of the same. The study is based on the secondary sources, some case studies of the past, and on review-based dimensions. Official documents, lessons learnt in the past missions, and expert opinions have been used to arrive at possible deductions.

Causes of Hostage Situation

The field of hostage-taking falls within the preview of conflict theory and conflict management. Managing a hostage crisis is also a conflict resolution in a crisis situation (Vecchi, et al., 2005). Conflict is the perceived blocking of important goals, needs, or interests of one person or group by another person or group. In the last five decades, hostage taking situations have rapidly come to the center-stage due to ever present threat of insurgencies or terrorism, tremendous loss of lives, and ever-increasing role of omni-present media. Control over the political narrative, religious interpretation discourses, and socio-economic allurements remain the main causes of conflicts. The goals of hostage takers are generally to gain political, criminal, and/or social benefits through a coercive or forced situation (Hancerli, 2005). The preference for a settlement by all parties is always with the commencement of negotiations, while preparing for tactical interventions or defence. All states will have varying strategies in a hostage situation, from no negotiation to a varying degree of expert or mediation parleys.

Amongst many notable crises, Moscow theatre hostage of 2002 and Beslan school siege of 2004 are remembered as bloody interventions by the state. Other notable hostage episodes go back to the Munich Olympic Games of 1972, Iranian Embassy Siege, 1980, and Branch of Davidians Barricade in Waco, 1993. Closer home, Mumbai Taj Mahal hotel seize of 2008 comes to mind. While tackling a hostage situation, any loss of hostage lives come under a huge criticism by the media, public, and the government. Many people lost their lives due to bad planning or rushed jobs in the past. According to studies by Michalowski et al (1988), some of the past application of force to the situations has not been entirely successful in saving hostages' lives and terrorists have succeeded in achieving their political objectives.

Terrorism is an asymmetric warfare and none of the international humanitarian laws or international rules applies to them, though the governments are required to follow these. Scenarios of hostage taking differ with the motives as taking hostages or commandeering a ship or an aircraft, may be intended to exchange the captured goods or persons or simply extorting money or logistics (Hancerli, 2005). But a 'no communication' from hostage-takers can also mean the intent of being punitive or revengeful. In such a case, negotiations require convincing the hostage-takers to commence negotiations. Negotiation is a discreet form of diplomacy at most of the places, especially in case of hostage taking with punitive motives (Faure, 2008). Here, the negotiators engage in a very peculiar type of diplomacy even when the official line is to not to negotiate with a terrorist. Negotiator needs to be a good listener and learn to demonstrate empathy and understanding of the problems, needs, and issues of others. Only then can one hope to influence their behaviour in a positive way (Thompson, 2016). National policies range from 'No Negotiation' to the 'Track II Negotiation'. These may also take a form of 'Regular Negotiation' or a 'Negotiation in order to Prepare for an Assault'. No negotiation is a policy followed by the most Western countries and is often applied during a hostage crisis. Often the policy is limited to not paying ransom demands, and doesn't apply to other forms of negotiation (Meyer, 2013). All of these have a direct relevance to the UN PK scenarios.

Causes of Conflicts in UN Peacekeeping

UN PK is a sub-text of the social upheavals and on-going conflicts across various nations. Peace operations result in mostly from negotiated settlements where all or most major parties to a conflict agree to negotiate and abide by a peace deal. Intra-state conflicts are political in nature and almost always a struggle to control the state's natural resources and political seat of power. The ideological conflicts influenced by the cold-war rivalries have reduced but powerful war-lords are still influenced by the major players of a region. Basic tenets of Peace Operations are consent, impartiality, and non-use of force except in self-defence and defence of the mandate (UN, 2021). PK is the deployment of a UN presence in the field with the consent of all the parties concerned (Boutros-Ghali, 1992). Some of these principles are largely compromised by one or other party, immediately after a PK mission commences in its area. In spite of all the critics, there are numerous positive outcomes of peace operations to most of the stakeholders, when it is maintained under the basic principles. However, consent remains a fluid concept and parties to the conflict stick to it depending on their self-interests.

Fjelde et al. (2019) carried out an empirical study on the reduction in violence and protection of civilians with the deployment of UN peacekeepers in Africa. The study found that UN deployments in areas which had seen violence against civilians, and in rebel held areas, reduced the risk of violence against civilians by rebel actors. However, the UN was less effective in hindering violence by the government forces. The inference was that reliance on government consent made peacekeepers less willing to impose military and political costs on the government actors in the areas of their deployment.

It is well documented that peace operations do not generate only positive and beneficial outcomes, but can also have negative consequences as explained in Unintended Consequences of Peacekeeping (Aoi, Coning, & Thakur, 2007). Peace operations tend to distort the host economy, bring in immoral activities like human trafficking, prostitution, smuggling and gun-running. Slowly, the PK force leans towards the most cooperating faction(s) or state, thus, setting a stage for antagonism from the other factions. Aoi et al. (2007) have termed the philosophical debate on unintended consequences related ethical issues, as "double effect" debate. Double effects are both positive and negative consequences of peacekeepers' actions.

The conflicts in UN Operations with the antagonists have resulted in heavy losses to the peacekeepers. UN Fatality figures of 4103, as on 31 May 2021, largely represent accidents, illnesses and malicious acts. Out of these, top 15 PK missions with malicious acts (1016 fatalities) related to hostile actions against the peacekeepers are as given below:

1. Mali (MINUSMA) - 144
2. Congo 1960-64 (ONUC) - 35

3. Somalia (UNOSOM) - 114

4. Lebanon (UNIFIL) - 93

5. Congo (MONUC+MONUSCO) - 74

6. Former Yugoslavia (UNPROFOR) - 74

7. Darfur (UNAMID) - 73

8. Central Africa (MINUSCA) - 48

9. Sinai (UNEF I & II) - 35

10. Cambodia (UNTAC) - 25

11. Palestine (UNTSO) - 26

12. Sierra Leone (UNMASIL) - 17

13. Cyprus (UNFICYP) - 15

14. South Sudan (UNMISS) - 14

15. Rwanda (UNAMIR) - 14

Wesley, (1995) has claimed that hostage effect has remained a grey area in peacekeeping where peacekeepers' inherent vulnerability is used for influencing decisions by the belligerents. The study is in the background of Bosnian crises and the author explored the sources and operation of the hostage effect with three case studies: ONUSAL, a functioning hostage effect; UNOSOM II, a dysfunctional hostage effect; and UNPROFOR II, a malfunctioning hostage effect. The conclusions suggested significant ramifications for the applicability of peacekeeping depending on a conflict situation. The UN data does not specifically mention the hostage taking and related fatalities, but can be analysed from mission reports. Every hostage situation is unique because there are different motivations, demands, deadlines, and actors involved.

Nygren (2019) studied the behaviour of rebels in attacking and hostage-taking of UN peacekeepers and concluded that when rebels were within their stronghold, the capabilities made them stronger than the existing government forces, which prompted such actions. Rebels attack peacekeepers only as a strategic move with a clear political intent. They are always looking at leveraging their strength to increase their bargaining range against a perceived injustice or partiality of the UN (Fjelde et al., 2019).

Every situation would require a different line of action and final resolution. For the UN, situation is more complex as besides the UN HQ, both the DPO and DPPA, Force HQ in the mission area and TCCs are actively engaged in the process, mostly with differing agendas. However, past experiences in UN PK scenarios have proved that the formulating of negotiation strategies and preparation to use force at the appropriate time are the most likely outcomes of such deliberations. Unified resolutions for handling hostage situations increase the credibility and reliability of the force on ground. Time is of critical importance and for that, structured negotiation plays an important part. What is at stake is usually highly dramatic as one is dealing with human lives. Thus, the smallest mistakes can result in terrible consequences for the hostages and the UN force on the field. The situation is characterised by uncertainties which include the credibility of the demands and degree of threat. Freeing the hostages from their captors will always pose unique operational challenges as any use of force may likely be retaliated.

Some Cases of Hostage Situations

> ➢ Cambodia - Dec 1992. The reluctant party to the agreement, Khmer Rouge started withdrawing its tactical consent as soon as electoral process started. This also resulted in their taking many peacekeepers hostage at various places. Many were held up for a day

or more, but more serious situation was in a province, where they were stronger. Six UN military observers were held for three days in appalling conditions. Their release was secured through negotiations in mixed military working groups at force HQ and provincial levels. On 08 April 1993, one day into the election campaign, a Japanese electoral supervisor and his Khmer interpreter were killed, leading to almost a collapse of electoral supervisory force (Findlay, 1995).

➢ Rwanda - 1994. The presidential guard captured the 10 Belgian peacekeeping troops from UNAMIR, who had been protecting the country's Prime Minister, Madame Uwilingiyimana. Five Ghanaian soldiers who were quickly set free. The other ten were Belgians from the Para commando Brigade, and were tortured and hacked to death with machetes (Melvern, 2004). Maj Bernard Ntuyanhaga was held responsible by a Belgian Court and sentenced to 20 years prison term.

➢ Bosnia - 1995. Bosnian Serbs took more than 450 U.N. troops hostage at different locations in May-June 1995 after their ammunition dumps were bombed by the NATO planes. The Serbs took UN hostages, holding many of them as human shields. The hostages were held for weeks. The Bosnian Serbs also held 30 UN military observers, many tied to poles or potential targets of NATO air strikes. French hostages on a bridge proved to be one of the major clash points, where the French used force and freed their soldiers (CIA, 2002; pp. 312-313). A classic case of disaster due to Chapter VII/enforcement action by the NATO, from air and UN peacekeeping at ground.

➢ Angola - 1998. 3 members of the UN Observer Mission in Angola (MONUA) held by UNITA rebels.

These were predominantly Indian nationals. Released successfully and both the UN and UNITA claimed that they were not held hostages.

➢ Sierra Leone - 2000. Rebel, RUF forces had political ambition and wanted to retain their hold on the rich diamond business in cohort with the Liberians and Nigerians. Rebels in Sierra Leone held more than 300 U.N. troops and military observers as hostage for over two months, besides disarming and marching scores others to Liberia. Four U.N. soldiers from Kenya were killed and eight wounded. RUF forces disarmed and detained a contingent of 208 troops from Zambia who were on their way to the northern town of Makeni (Raman, 2000). The crisis for Indian company at Kailhun ended with military operation 'Khukhri' undertaken by the Indian troops.

➢ Golan Heights - 2013. 21 U.N. peacekeepers held hostage for four days. By the Martyrs of the Yarmouk Brigades asking for the Syrian troops to withdraw from the area. Both Fijian and Pilipino peacekeepers were held hostages at different time frames. The causes could be attributed to make a political statement of their clout against on-going fight with the Syrian Government forces and engaging UN into their struggles.

➢ South Sudan - 2015. 18 UNMISS uniformed peacekeepers (Bangladesh) taken hostage in South Sudan. 12 South Sudanese contractors working with the peacekeepers were taken hostage with a motive to disrupt supply lines and capture fuel and arms (UN News Oct., 2015). All were released after confiscating all the material supplies.

Force Protection and Negotiation

Based on the experiences of UN peace operations, emphasis on force protection measures and robust rules of engagement have been given due attention in modern PK operations. Even the mandates are made robust which allow the peacekeepers use of force dependent on the operational requirement. Besides the armed units, UN PKOs also have unarmed military observers, UN civilians or police personnel. The UN has some force protection or International Convention against the Taking of Hostages declarations but eventual preventive actions are left to the local leadership of a PK force (Willmot, Sheeran, & Sharland, 2015). Substantial analysis of UN safety and security issues has occurred since 2003, following the bombing of the UN headquarters in Iraq, and the system has made efforts to improve and strengthen its security policies and arrangements. However, security issues are often perceived as primarily technical matters and are not prioritised as strategically or politically important despite their centrality to the effectiveness of peace operations.

Response of the UN to hostage-taking is not uniform and at best adhoc. The deficits in a cohesive and coordinated approach have been identified in various studies and reports of special representatives of the UN Secretary General and the force commanders since 1992. Brahimi report identified lack of coordination and planning of the PK Operations. The UN repeatedly failed to meet the challenges as per the report (Brahimi, 2000). Underfunding of Missions such as in Bosnia, Somalia, and Sierra Leone was pointed out as one of the main observations of failure.

Some Existing International Guidelines

> ➢ Practice Relating to Rule 96. Hostage-Taking. IHL. Article 4(2) (c) of the 1977 Additional Protocol II states that the taking of hostages is prohibited.

- ➢ International Convention against the Taking of Hostages. The 1979 International Convention against the Taking of Hostages criminalizes hostage-taking. Article 1 provides: Any person who seizes or detains and threatens to kill, to injure or to continue to detain another person (hereinafter referred to as "hostage") in order to compel a third party, namely, a State, an international intergovernmental organisation, a natural or juridical person, or a group of persons to do or to abstain from doing any act as an explicit or implicit condition for the release of the hostage, commits the offence of taking of hostages.

- ➢ Hostage Survival Skills for Canadian Forces Personnel by Maj Murphy and Capt. Farley. Types, situations, reaction from panic to Stockholm Syndrome. Survival guidelines. (Canadian Institute of Strategic Studies).

- ➢ Calhoun: The NPS Institutional Archive, Naval Postgraduate School. Major Perez (2004), Anatomy of a hostage rescue: what makes hostage rescue operations successful? Principles, processes, and operational aspects of dealing with a hostage situation.

- ➢ Lessons Learned in Peacekeeping Operations: The Ad Hoc Group on Cooperation in Peacekeeping was established within the framework of NACC in 1993.

- ➢ UNSMS Security Policy Manual – Hostage Incident Management. Promulgated on 15 April 2012. The purpose of this policy is to outline the UNSMS strategy and approach to managing the risk from hostage-taking. In the Field Security Handbook (2006).

- ➢ Safe and Secure Approaches in Field Environments

(SSAFE) Training. Eight standard training modules - UN Security Management System (UNSMS); History, Background and Culture; Radio Communications; Personal Security; Weapons Awareness; Travel, Convoy and Vehicle Security; Hostage Survival and Incident Management and Basic Life Support.

- ➢ UN Peacekeeping PDT Standards, Specialized Training Material for Military Experts on Mission 1st Edition 2010.

- ➢ High level Independent Panel on Peace Operations 2014. Report in 2015. A comprehensive assessment of the state of UN peace operations today, and the emerging needs of the future

- ➢ Improving the safety of UN Peacekeepers Report – 2017. The committee reviewed nine casualty-related databases; 43 mission senior leadership end of mission reports; 97 Board of Inquiry reports; 11 military and police assessment reports of the DPKO; special investigation reports (UNMISS); and numerous academic and 'think tank' publications. The committee also conducted over 160 interviews of senior leadership, mid-level staff and technical experts at HQ and the field; and consultations with representatives of Member States; and three academic, research institutions and subject-matter experts. The report is comprehensive and may be further evaluated and used for force protection measures. The UN and TCCs are, still gripped by a "Chapter VI Syndrome."

- ➢ Improving Security of UN Peacekeepers (09 April 2018): Action Plan for implementation of fatalities report. At field and headquarters level. Changing mindset, improved capacity, threat-oriented footprint and accountability.

Possible steps for Policy Framing

- ➢ Data base be established to understand hostage takers' approaches and UN applications to negotiation. This will give a broader understanding of the components of hostage situations. Need to establish expertise at UN HQ and Force HQ levels linked to this data base.

- ➢ Establishment of mission working groups at political and military/police level at each Force HQ. Cooperation will help improve resolutions and cease situations without losing hostages.

- ➢ Force protection should be in built into the mission mandate. Adequate rapid reaction force to contain an area. Each unit and region be aware of the possible scenarios.

- ➢ Read and implement the Report of 2017, which blames inaction as the primary reason of violence against the UN components in a mission area. The report recommends that "the UN should identify threats to their security and take the initiative, using all the tactics, to neutralize or eliminate the threats. Missions should go where the threat is, in order to neutralize it."

Conclusion

Some authors also question the idea of international interventions at all. Weinstein (2005) of Stanford University provided a theory of "autonomous recovery," in which states can achieve sustainable peace without international intervention. Uganda, Eritrea, and Somalia, demonstrate effective institutions coming out of warfare. UN or other intervention can stop mass atrocities, but also stop institutional change. Autonomous recovery elevates the strongest leader, but also rewards the strongest fighters who may be less inclined to share power. International relations theories – realism, critical security studies, practice theory, and complexity theory – can be applied to a specific policy issue. Applying these theories enhances our understanding of why UN peacekeeping, as an international institution, has evolved in a particular direction and functions the way that it does. Conflict prevention and mediation must be brought back to the fore. Protection of civilians is a core obligation of the UN, but expectations and capability must converge. TCCs must equip their forces to take on mid-range threats and be ready to accept some fatalities in the process. The UN must have a comprehensive set of policy guidelines and force composition based on the realistic threat assessment.

References

Aoi, C., Coning, C., & Thakur, R. (Ed., 2007). Unintended consequences of peacekeeping operations. UNU Press, Tokyo.

Boutros-Ghali, B. (1992). An Agenda for Peace: Preventive Diplomacy, Peacemaking and Peace-keeping. International Relations, 11(3), 201–218. https://doi. org/10.1177/004711789201100302

Bove, V., & Elia, L. (2011). Supplying Peace: Participation in and Troop Contribution to Peacekeeping Missions. Journal of Peace Research 48 (6):699–714.

Bove, V., & Ruggeri, A. (2015). Kinds of Blue: Diversity in UN Peacekeeping Missions and Civilian Protection. B.J.Political Science. 46, 681–700

Brahimi, L. (2000). Report of the Panel on United Nations Peace Operations. Available at: https://www.un.org/en/events/ pastevents/brahimi_report.shtml

CIA (2002). Balkan Battlegrounds, Vol-I. CIA, Office of Russian and European Analysis, Washington.

Enders, W., & Sandler, T. (2006). The political economy of terrorism. Cambridge University Press.

Faure, G. O. (2008). Negotiating with Terrorists: A Discrete Form of Diplomacy. The Hague Journal of Diplomacy, 3; 179-200.

Findlay, T. (1995). Cambodia: The legacy and lessons of UNTAC. SIPRI Research Report No 9. Oxford Press.

Fjelde, H., Hultman, L. & Nilsson, D. (2019). Protection through presence: UN peacekeeping and the costs of targeting civilians. International Organization 73, 103–31. doi:10.1017/S0020818318000346

Hancerli, S.(2005). Toward successful negotiation strategies in hostage situations: Case study approach and future recommendations. Master's Thesis University Of North Texas. Retrieved from: https://digital.library.unt.edu/ark:/67531/metadc4811/m2/1/high_res_d/thesis.pdf

Kseniya, O, & John, K. (2020). United Nations Peace Operations and International Relations Theory: An Introduction. United Nations Peace Operations and International Relations Theory, 2020, Available at SSRN: https://ssrn.com/abstract=3665340

Licklider, R. (1995). Stopping the killing: How civil wars end. The Journal of Politics; 57, (1). 297-299. https://doi.org/10.2307/2960302

Melvern, L (2004). Conspiracy to Murder: The Rwandan Genocide, Verso: New York, ISBN 1-85984-588-6.

Meyer, J. (2013). Why the G8 pact to stop paying terrorist ransoms probably won't work- and isn't even such a great idea. Quartz. Retrieved from https://qz.com/95618/why-the-g8-pact-to-stop-paying-terrorist-ransoms-probably-wont-work-and-isnt-even-such-a-great-idea/

Michalowski, Kersten, Koperczak, Matvin, Szpakowicz & Connolly (1988).

Nygren, E (2019). Violence against peacekeepers as a strategy:

Why rebel groups attack peacekeepers at some locations, and not others. Thesis for Department of Peace and Conflict Research, Uppsala University, Sweden.

Raman, A. (2000). Operation Khukri : Joint Excellence. USI Journal. Retreived from https://vayu-sena.tripod.com/other-unamsil-opkhukri.html

Roberts, A. (1994). The crisis in UN peacekeeping. Global Politics and Strategy 36 (3). Retrieved from https://doi.org/10.1080/00396339408442752

Thompson, J (2016). Crisis Negotiation: Understanding and using the skills of negotiators. NYPD, Hostage Negotiation Team. Retrieved from: https://www.adr.gov/pdf/IADRWG-may2016.pdf

Urquhart, B. (1993), The Future of Peace-keeping. Conference paper at LHE, June 1993 Oslo; Symposium on Collective Responses to Common Threats.

UN SMS (2011). UN Security Management System: Security Manual System. Available at https://www.un.org/sites/un2.un.org/files/undss-security_policy_manual_e-book.pdf

UN (2021). Principles of Peacekeeping. Retrieved from: https://peacekeeping.un.org/en/principles-of-peacekeeping

UN DPO (2017). Improving Security of United Nations Peacekeepers: We need to change the way we are doing business. High Level Panel Report, UN DPO. Available at: https://peacekeeping.un.org/sites/default/files/improving_security_of_ united_nations_peacekeepers_report.pdf

UN DPO (2021). UN Peacekeeping – Fatalities. Available at: https://peacekeeping.un.org/en/fatalities

UN News (Oct 2015). Head of mission urges release of remaining UN personnel taken hostage in South Sudan. Retrieved from: https://news.un.org/en/story/2015/10/514162-head-mission-urges-release-remaining-un-personnel-taken-hostage-south-sudan

Vecchi, G. M., Van Hasselt, V. B., & Romano, S. J. (2005). Crisis (hostage) negotiation: Current strategies and issues in high-risk conflict resolution. Aggression and Violent Behavior, 10, 533-551.

Van Der Lijn, V., & Smit, T. (2015). Peacekeepers under Threat? Fatality trends in UN peace operations. SIPRI Policy paper. Available at: https://www.sipri.org/sites/default/files/files/misc/SIPRIPB1509.pdf

Weinstein J (2005). Disentangling the Determinants of Successful Demobilization and Reintegration - Working Paper 69. Centre for Global Development. Available at: https://www.cgdev.org/publication/disentangling-determinants-successful-demobilization-and-reintegration-working-paper-69

Wesley, M. (1995). Blue Berets or blindfolds? Peacekeeping and the hostage Effect, International Peacekeeping, 2; 4, 457- 482, DOI: 10.1080/13533319508413575

Wilmot, H., Sheeran, S., & Sharland, L. (2015). Safety and Security Challenges in UN Peace Operations. New York: International Peace Institute.

Strategy & Challenges of Hostage Rescue when Peacekeepers from larger TCCs are taken Hostage (UNAMSIL)

Lieutenant General Vijay Kumar Jetley,
PVSM, UYSM (Retd)

Introduction

This is a story of an ill-fated UN Mission created at the turn of the century for the purpose of keeping the peace in strife-torn Sierra Leone. On reaching Sierra Leone, this UN mission, UNAMSIL, discovered to its horror that the peace holding the country together was a tenuous one. This tiny country is located on the West coast of the African continent, circular in shape and wedged between Guinea to its North and East; Liberia to its East and South and the Atlantic Ocean to its South-West and West. It has one of the largest reserves of rich minerals like diamonds, gold, silver and rutile which ordinarily should be a boon for any country. Yet, these very resources were its bane mainly because the copious wealth, particularly of diamonds, attracted the attention of many unscrupulous elements that coveted these resources. Abject poverty, under-development, and corrupt governments were the catalysts that made Sierra Leone the ideal breeding ground that gave birth to many bands of blood-thirsty rebels that waged war against the legally constituted governments of the day, ironically using the abundant diamond reserves

to finance and fuel their reprehensible activities. This hapless nation was the victim of a long civil war which had supposedly come to an end. However, this was only on paper as events that unfolded subsequently proved.

Prevailing Situation

Over the years, many rebel groups cropped up in Sierra Leone and each vying not only for the mineral wealth of the country but harbouring the desire to rule the country. Internecine fighting between the various rebel groups and factions was common place. At times, foes became friends to fight against the government of the day. The main rebel group was the Revolutionary United Front (RUF). On the other hand, a shaky balance of power was created by the pro-government rebel groups called the Civil Defence Forces (CDF) that formed their own vigilante groups. In late 1999, the CDF numbered around 4000 rebels.

Civil war waged in the country for over a decade in the 1990s. To bring hostilities to an end, the government signed the Abidjan Accord with the RUF in November 1996 but this accord failed miserably. By this time, Sierra Leone had become a country stretched beyond its ability to effectively govern itself. A country that had more or less ceded control of its future to dissidents and rebels of all hues and colours. The unrest and instability generated by the civil war spilled over into the immediate neighbourhood which made West African States to sit up and take note. To suppress the unlawful activities of the rebels in Liberia, it was decided by the Economic Community of West African States (ECOWAS) and the UN to cobble together a peacekeeping force with troops mainly from the Nigerian Army. This force, called the Economic Community Military Observer Group (ECOMOG), was sent to Liberia to quell the unrest there. Once a semblance of order was restored in Liberia, ECOWAS was in a position to concentrate its full attention on Sierra Leone and, therefore, sent its force ECOMOG there for peacekeeping/peace enforcement.

Sierra Leone went through one crisis after another and by April 1998, ECOMOG, predominantly of Nigerian content, had 13 Nigerian Battalions, a Guinean battalion and a smaller number of troops from other West African States in Sierra Leone. Yet, due to many constraints and a number of other factors, ECOMOG did not maintain pressure on the rebels and lost the initiative, resulting in the horrendous attack by the RUF on the capital Freetown in December 1998/January 1999, with main attack on 6th and 7th of January 1999.

As all the agreements signed thus far had failed to produce positive results, thus, the idea of making a fresh effort in this regard was born resulting in the antagonists being made to agree to the evolution and signing of the Lome Peace Agreement on 07 July 1999, wherein the Government of Sierra Leone (GOSL), headed by President Ahmed Tejan Kabbah on the one hand and the leader of the rebel faction the RUF, headed by Corporal Foday Sankoh, on the other came to terms with each other and decided to together form a Government of National Unity (GNU). Essentially, the Agreement called for a permanent and a total cessation of hostilities. The government and the representatives of the RUF were to be part of governance and the Disarmament, Demobilisation and Reintegration (DDR) programme for all rebels was to commence immediately.

UN Efforts

A neutral Peacekeeping Force consisting of the existing ECOMOG with two additional battalions was to continue to remain in Sierra Leone with the mandate to maintain peace and security as well as to provide protection to the personnel deployed to oversee the implementation of this Agreement with particular reference to the security of those entrusted with the responsibility of conducting the DDR programme. However, by September 1999, barely two months after the signing of the Lome Peace Agreement, Nigeria, one of the major signatories to the Lome Peace Agreement, expressed a desire to quit Sierra Leone. It is pertinent to note here that 13 of the 15 battalions comprising ECOMOG, which was mandated to ensure maintenance of peace and security in Sierra Leone post the Agreement, were from Nigeria. This spurred the UN to create another international peacekeeping Force called UNAMSIL, to work in conjunction with a scaled down ECOMOG and assist in the DDR programme. Both the Forces had different mandates.

UNAMSIL consisted of six infantry battalions with supporting arms and services. Four of these battalions were to be inducted into UNAMSIL from out of the ECOMOG, two battalions from Nigerian, one battalion from Ghana and one battalion from Guinea. Unfortunately, all four battalions were highly deficient of essential weapons and equipment, besides being ill trained and badly led, resulting in their being operationally unfit and ineffective. The other two battalions were one each from Kenya and India; thankfully, both these battalions were well equipped.

The mandate given to UNAMSIL was a peacekeeping one, basically to work under the provisions of Chapter VI of the UN Charter, which entailed peaceful negotiations with the rebels to encourage them to join the DDR programme. However, it had windows of Chapter VII that permitted use of force under certain circumstances. Hence, it was a robust mandate that was made clear to the nations contributing troops to UNAMSIL. Rules of Engagement (ROE) further clarified this. Yet, most troops comprising UNAMSIL were loath to use force whenever the need for the same arose. Resultantly, this emboldened the rebels, particularly the RUF, who, despite having got a fantastic deal in the Lome Peace Agreement including blanket pardon and amnesty for all past crimes and the chance of becoming part of the government, continued to remain belligerent and retained their weapons. The hesitation and vacillation of UNAMSIL troops in the face of the rebels was to have dire consequences subsequently as the Saga of Sierra Leone brings out.

By December 1999, as the pressure on the UN to absorb ECOMOG into the fold of the UN was not working out, Nigeria firmed up its decision to pull out from Sierra Leone, leaving UNAMSIL with just six battalions to not only do justice to its own mandate but also to take over the responsibilities of ECOMOG.

The unthinkable happened on 01 May 2000, when RUF rebels attacked the Kenyan troops at Makeni. A quick operational plan was put into action that succeeded admirably in relieving pressure on the Kenyan troops deployed at Makeni and Magburaka, however, the newly inducted Zambian battalion that was to deliver the killer punch got itself tricked into captivity without firing a single shot. By the evening of 03 May 2000, the RUF had taken almost the entire Zambian battalion as hostage. Simultaneously, to the attack on the peacekeepers at Makeni, as part of a clearly well orchestrated game plan, RUF rebels surrounded two companies of Indian peacekeepers deployed in the eastern part of the country at a place called Kailahun. But they refrained from attacking the Indian peacekeepers as the rebels knew that the Indian peacekeepers were no pushovers and, hence, the two Indian companies continued to hold off the rebels for 75 days until a rescue operation called Operation Khukri was launched. The Mission at this stage was in shambles and steps had to be taken to prevent its collapse.

By the end of the third day after the attack on Makeni, the RUF had taken approximately 500 peacekeepers as hostages while another 250 plus were in a stand-off at a place called Kailahun in the east. Action had to be taken to set things right, however, there were no resources with UNAMSIL at this juncture to plan any bold action. To understand what we did, it is best to divide the hostages into three categories.

Categorisation and Rescue of Hostages

To understand how the hostages were rescued it became necessary to categorise them into three categories as under:-

(a) Category 1 peacekeepers were those that were forced on threat of violence to give up their weapons and equipment to the rebels and were then forced out of their deployment areas and permitted to deploy elsewhere. These were basically the Nigerians troops who surrendered their weapons and equipment to the RUF rebels at Kambia and were permitted to redeploy at Port Loko.

(b)   Category 2 peacekeepers were those that had an encounter with the RUF, resulting in the weapons and equipment of the peacekeepers being forcibly snatched from them. Thereafter, such peacekeepers were captured and taken to different locations by the rebels. These included the bulk of the Zambian battalion, the Kenyan Sector HQ and some Kenyans missing since the outbreak of hostilities at Makeni and Magburaka. Also three MILOBs from the Makeni team site.

(c)   Category 3 peacekeepers were those that were surrounded by the rebels but never gave up their weapons and equipment and stood fast in a stand-off with the rebels, not giving an inch to the rebels. These included the Indian Battalion (INDBATT) troops at Kailahun and those that were surrounded at Kuiva.

Rescue of Category 1 peacekeepers posed no problem at all as the issue was over before its impact could be felt. The 'capture' of such peacekeepers; the confiscation of their weapons and the lack of violence against the Nigerian peacekeepers, all appeared to be part of an elaborate charade put up in connivance with the RUF by Brigadier M A Garba, the Deputy Force Commander (DFC), perhaps with support of Mr Adenji, the Special Representative of the Secretary General (SRSG) and the Head of the Mission. The return of the weapons and equipment of the Nigerians and their release from Kambia the very next day was negotiated by the DFC with the leader of the RUF, Foday Sankoh.

The plight of the Category 2 peacekeepers caused us maximum anxiety as their safety was endangered. They were ill fed, malnourished, and often ill-treated. A Gambian military observer shattered his leg when the UN vehicle, being driven by a rebel, in which he was travelling met with an accident. He did not get proper medical treatment until his repatriation roughly six weeks later. The repatriation of these hostages was organised through the good offices of the President of Liberia Mr Charles Taylor, the appointed interlocutor between the rebels and UNAMSIL. The reason for this was because Taylor had direct links with the RUF rebels and often called them over to his capital Monrovia to interact with them and give them his 'advice' and 'directions'. In fact, it was an open secret that after the capture and incarceration of Foday Sankoh in a jail in Freetown, Taylor was the de facto head of the RUF. Despite being appointed as the interlocutor and mediator, Taylor was criticised by many nations because of his collusion with the rebels. He was even accused of actually directing RUF operations against UNAMSIL. However, the fact of the matter was that had he not been asked to intervene, we would not have got back all the hostages from the clutches of the rebels. All this took considerable time to bring about but that was only to be expected.

In addition to the efforts of the interlocutor, efforts for the release of the captured peacekeepers were made by:-

(a) ECOWAS - by the Heads of West African States.

(b) Organisation of Afracian Union (OAU).

(c) Affected nations like Kenya, Zambia and India contacted the President of   Liberia directly.

(d) Our Prime Minister Mr Vajpayee spoke directly

with Mr Kofi Annan, the Secretary General, with the President of Nigeria, Liberia and Sierra Leone.

(e)   Ambassador Dinkar Srivastava, JS (UNP), came to Sierra Leone and was a great help in sorting things out. Our ambassador in Ivory Coast also negotiated directly with President Charles Taylor for the lifting of the cordon around the Indian peacekeepers at Kailahun.

(f)   India also sent the DGMO, Gen Vij to seek the support of USA and UK but he could make no headway as they refused to participate in any rescue operations

Taylor was embroiled in many controversies but remained unaffected because criticisms to him were like water off a ducks back. He was very clear about what and why he was doing what he was doing. His actions were not altruistic by any stretch of imagination. On one hand, he was doing a great favour to the international community in general and to the UN in particular by organising the release of the peacekeepers captured by the RUF. He was clever enough to know that he was the only one who had the influence over the RUF to bring this about. He also knew that the international community understood this but it least bothered him. His aim appeared to be to get in the good books of the international community and then to use the influence of the US, UK and the others to get his good friend Foday Sankoh released from jail. On the other hand, he was not doing this interlocution gratis for the RUF. He was giving impression to the RUF cadre in the field that he was fighting for the release of their leader Sankoh, he was surely demanding diamonds in return for his effort. Sir Jeremy Greenstock of UK had earlier pointed to the need to discuss regional aspects of the conflict in Sierra Leone, particularly the role of Liberia. "There is growing evidence that diamonds are leaving Sierra Leone illegally via Liberia, and arms are coming into the RUF, and perhaps others, illegally from Liberia."

The last set of peacekeepers whose safety was a cause of concern were those at Kailahun and Kuiva. However, as the peacekeepers at Kailahun were in sufficient numbers and had BRDMs (a kind of wheeled Armoured Vehicle) with a high rate of fire, plus determined troops that were capable of defending themselves in case the RUF became violent, the concern for their safety was not as acute as the concern for the safety of the 23 peacekeepers captured and held hostage by them at Kuiva as they were definitely vulnerable being outnumbered by the rebels. The saving grace was that since initially the RUF had not divested them of their weapons, it was a sort of an indicator that the RUF did not have any aggressive designs against them for the moment. But this was not an assurance of the continued good behaviour of the RUF rebels. Strictly speaking, the peacekeepers at these two locations could not be called hostages, at least not as yet. Their situation, at best, could be described as being in a 'stand-off' with the RUF with everything intact. On the plus side was the fact that due to the healthy respect that the rebels had for the Indian peacekeepers, movement of food convoys, as also key personnel, had been permitted, at least up to 04 June 2000. The company commander and Regimental Medical Officer (RMO) at Kailahun were permitted to visit the peacekeepers that were moved from Kuiva to Pendembu. This was done on the basis of an unwritten honour code that permitted such visits on the premise that the company commander and the RMO would return back to Kailahun by the evening. Similarly, the 2IC held hostage along with 22 other peacekeepers was permitted to visit the Battalion HQ at Daru with the promise to return back to Kuiva by the evening. Consequently, there was no immediate threat to the peacekeepers at Kailahun and Kuiva.

Finally, as no headway was being made even after 70 days of the stand-off, I took the decision to launch Operation Khukri. I had sufficient troops by mid-June 2000 to plan this military operation. Time does not permit me to go into the details of this operation but suffice to say it was a multi-national, multi-dimensional and multi-directional one, on a very large scale, the type not seen in UN peacekeeping operations, and a very successful one. We had one fatal casualty and 6 to 7 wounded.

Conclusion

In the end, all that I would like to say is that peacekeeping is a very complex operation that cannot be done by everyone. A lot of training and preparation is required and peacekeepers should mentally be prepared to use force under Chapter VII of the UN Charter. This was one of the biggest drawbacks of the force in Sierra Leone as most of the troops shied away from use of force. And to use force, apart from guts and gumption, there is a requirement of well equipped, motivated, and trained troops led by fearless commanders and such troops are a rarity in the UN.

Strategy & Challenges of Hostage Rescue when Peacekeepers from TCCs are taken Hostage (UNDOF)

Lieutenant General IS Singha, AVSM, VSM (Retd)

Introduction

The Arab Spring that started in Tunisia in December 2010 spread to Syria in March 2011. By the end of the year, Free Syrian Army consisting mainly of deserters from the Syrian Army had started fighting with the Syrian Arab Armed Forces (SAAF) and the government supported militia. When I joined as the Head of the Mission and Force Commander at Golan Heights in August 2012, Armed Opposition Groups (AOGs) having allegiance to Free Syrian Army, Al Nusra and later ISIS had already entered the buffer zone between Israel and Syria called the Area of Separation (AOS), which, in a funnel shape, is ten km wide in the North and one km wide in the South. The SAAF also entered the buffer zone to engage these groups and some of the fighting used to spill over to the Israeli side, and the Israelis were extra vigilant but did not want to overtly get involved with the civil war in Syria. Seven out of ten times the Israelis did not retaliate if some bombs or rockets landed on their side but when they did, it was for effect and the weapon system on Syrian side was completely destroyed. Incidents of hostage taking of the Syrian Liaison Officers accompanying the peacekeepers and their eventual killings had taken place earlier in first half of 2012 thereby restricting our freedom of movement.

The first peacekeeper to be taken as hostage was my legal advisor, a French-Canadian, within two months of my joining and remained with the abductor armed group for nearly nine months. Unfortunately, the legal advisor did everything illegal by moving out of the camp alone, without permission, in a single vehicle, through a prohibited route which was dominated by the deadliest AOG called Al Nusra. This incident, however, gave me an opportunity to clamp down strict movement regulations wherein all moves were planned as convoy movement with protection.

A total of 180 peacekeepers were taken hostages in ten major incidents from 2012 to 2014 in Syria on Golan Heights. 150 of them were kept in custody of armed groups from 04 to 15 days and the balance 30 were released within few hours of their detention. We reacted with alacrity every time but each incident was handled differently. All hostages were released without loss of a single life due to good ground work for negotiations and expert hostages' crisis management. After we took some tough decisions and actions, hostage taking was averted for one year and three months, and recommenced only when ISIS and affiliated groups started targeting peacekeepers directly in August 2014. The size of the groups of hostages varied from 01 to 45. Finally in September 2014, we were able to move the entire mission safely onto the Israeli side through an improvised crossing point within a week without any violent incident.

AREA OF RESPONSIBILITY OF UNDOF

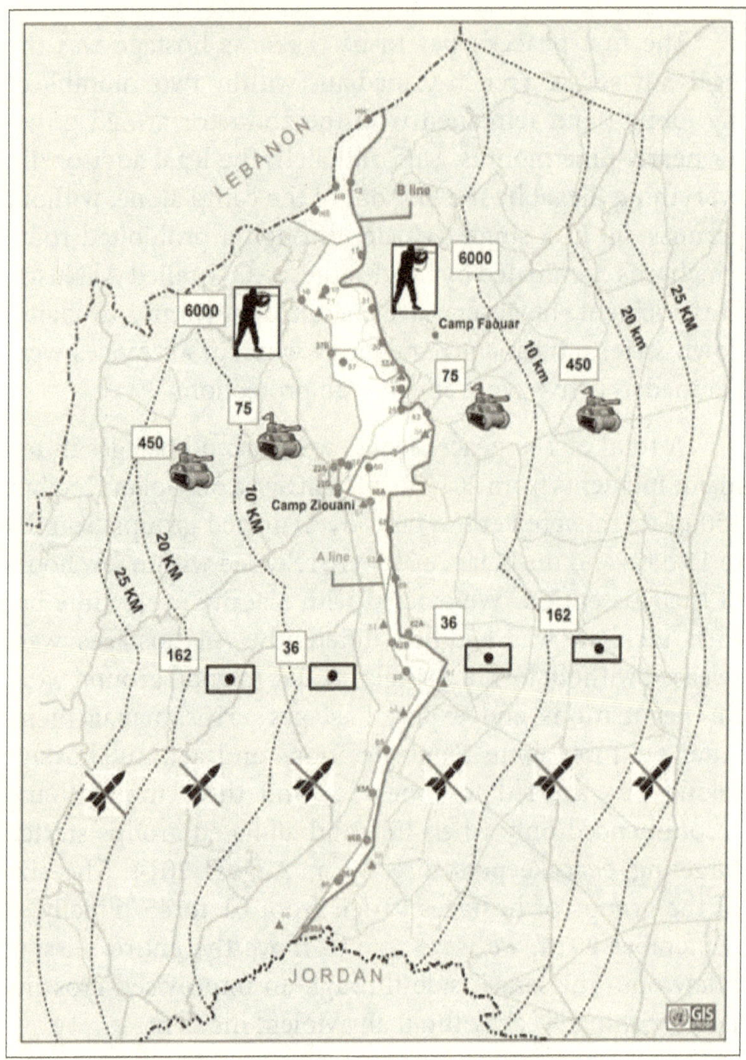

Prevailing Environment

There was bugger's muddle in the Buffer Zone where as per the 1974 Agreement, no armed elements from Syria or Israel were allowed to enter. Presence of over 30 AOGs and SAAF engaging them in the AOS (buffer zone) made peacekeeping very challenging. Peacekeepers were subjected to cross fire, abduction, weapon snatching, and carjacking. Our freedom of movement was severely restricted and we were denied access to the newly created bases of both the AOGs and the SAAF. We started having a major violent incident every week and we asked UN HQ for Capacity Building after carrying out a Mission Capability study.

Standard Operation Procedures (SOPs), drills and contingency plans were revised and rehearsed. As mentioned earlier, we resorted to organised, orderly, and planned convoy moves with protection to minimise cases of violence and abductions. Within two years, five out of the six original Troop Contributing Countries (TCCs) namely Canada, Japan, Croatia, Austria and Philippines pulled out their troops because of the security reasons. Only India stood fast and was joined by Nepal, Fiji, and Irelands as the new TCCs. I made it a point to flag at UN HQ, New York that the incoming TCCs should not have any caveats or restrictions on employment of their troops.

Aim of Abductors

Each armed group had its own agenda and a different orientation and motivation for taking hostages. The peacekeepers were taken as hostages mainly for attention seeking, looking for affiliation to ISIS & Al Nusra and getting funding, ransom, showing the Syrian government in bad light, and restricting the freedom of movement of UN peacekeepers.

Major Incidents of Hostages Crisis

There were five major and equal number of minor incidents of hostages taking in two years. The first one was along the Southern border with Jordon along the Yarmouk

River wherein the abductors captured four Philippino peacekeepers who were on a regular area domination patrol without weapons. The armed groups did not want any UN troops to come into the area of operations. The leader of the Yarmouk Brigade armed group was also seeking the release of his brother from a Jordanian jail which was not agreed to. Although we stopped patrolling this part of the border, we still had to maintain our southernmost position which was a section post of ten men at Position 86A.

The CO Philippino Battalion (Philbat) on 07 March 2013 planned to send a strong column of 22 armed peacekeepers for logistic maintenance of Position 86A, the southernmost position, in four armed vehicles. Unfortunately, clashes were taking place in the general area between SAAF and the AOGs and the rebel groups were under tremendous pressure to retreat. The rebel groups saw, stopped and checked our column on their way out and let them go. Probably in order to release the pressure from the SAAF, on the way back, our column was again challenged, their weapons and armed vehicles were taken away, and they were kept as hostages. This was the second major incident.

Some of the AOGs leaders carried the notion that we were assisting the SAAF with rations, water, arms and ammunition and accused the UN column of taking sides. Third reason was that these AOGs lived in tents and they found our Positions with pre-fabricated containers as attractive to convert into semi-permanent bases. Again, the demand of release of the brother of the leader from Jordanian jail was repeated. The deadly group Yarmouk Brigade, (abductor group), was also seeking the affiliation of ISIS which they achieved later after these two hostages' incidents.

First major incident of four philippino hostages

The Abductors from Yarmouk Brigade Group

The next major incident happened one year and three months later when the first Fiji Battalion had just been rotated. The AOGs attacked the Bravo Gate on the Syrian side of the only crossing place for UN peacekeepers between Syria and Israel at the abandoned city of Quneitra and captured it. They had attempted it one year earlier also but were not able to hold onto the captured area and were evicted by SAAF. However, that incident was the trigger for our oldest TCC Austria, who was the backbone of the mission, to pull out its troops from the mission. Therefore, to give depth to the gate area this time, they progressed their attack onto a SAAF company post in the old hospital building in the close vicinity of our company Position 27.

After the successful attack on SAAF post, the AOGs entered our post in search of water and food and found the position to be well stocked. They took all 45 Fijian soldiers as hostages and they were released after due deliberations in two weeks. While the Fijians were still in custody, the rebel groups surrounded Positions No 68 and 69 with 40 and 32 Phillipino soldiers in the two posts respectively. The armed groups asked our troops to surrender and handover their weapons. Negotiations were already on for release of Fijian troops but the armed groups told us that both cases were to be negotiated separately.

45 Fijians taken hostages in August 2014

While negotiations were ongoing, I had ordered the move of two troops of the newly arrived APC based Irish Force Reserve Company to move to Position 80 in the South from the Israeli side. Position 80 was in close proximity of Position 69 where 32 peacekeepers were held as hostages. On the third night, we noticed some movement of armed groups who had thinned out from the cordon around Position 69 and had strengthened the cordon around position 68. Finding a weakness and a gap, I ordered the Force Reserve Company located at Position 80 to evict peacekeepers from Position 69 in the wee hours of the morning. The rebel groups were caught off guard and we were able to evacuate 32 peacekeepers without a shot being fired.

Position 68 with 40 peacekeepers continued to be under tighter cordon. For two days, exchange of fire continued day and night between peacekeepers and the armed groups surrounding them. At the end of the day's negotiations on day four, at 5 PM, I was able to secure a ceasefire till 9 AM next morning and with suppressive artillery support from

Syrian Army and the fire being directed by Israeli officers, peacekeepers from position 68 found an escape route and crossed over to the Israeli side.

Next day when negotiations recommenced, I found our interlocutor was not in the picture that all Phillipino peacekeepers had escaped during the night. He was very upset and closed the negotiations about the release of Fijians. When the negotiations restarted, the armed groups asked us for blood money for three of their cadres killed by the peacekeepers. We apologised for the sad loss of lives in the exchange of fire but politely declined to any payments as it was against the fundamentals of United Nations peacekeeping. After 15 days in the custody, the 45 Fijians were released and handed over to us at Position 80.

Release of a US Journalist. The ISIS and affiliated groups had around 20 journalists taken as hostages and when they executed two of them, James Foley and Steven Sotloff, there was a lot of pressure on Obama administration to ensure the safe release of American journalists in custody of AOGs in Syria. One such journalist was released through our mission. I got a call directly from Secretary General's office and was requested to personally assist in the release of an American journalist by the name of Peter Theo Curtis. While the Omanis, and probably Qataris, did the track two diplomacy and prolonged negotiations with the AOG and their mentors, the Al Qaida associate group finally told them that they will only handover the hostage to Force Commander UNDOF at exactly the same location where they had handed over the Fijian soldiers (Position 80). The handover was planned for 10 AM but after prolonged negotiations, we were able to get the hostage by 6 PM in the evening. I made sure that the Indian doctor at the post carried out detailed medical inspection of the released journalist, before I handed him over to the US Ambassador to Israel, Daniel Shapiro.

Nuances of Negotiations and Handling of Hostages Crisis

Contingency Planning. We carried out revision of contingency planning and catered for nine contingencies to include Medical and Humanitarian Assistance to civilians, Action for Refuge Seekers, Freeing of Besieged Civilians, Camps for IDPs, Hostage Crisis, Actions on closing of the only Crossing Place between Syria and Israel, Evacuation and Relocation, Functioning on Pullout of a Major TCC and Protective Actions to deal with a Chemical Weapons Attack. We actually faced seven of these contingencies and had to take appropriate actions.

Preparatory Stage of Negotiations. Creating and maintaining contacts at different levels in the field is very important when the situation on the ground is dynamic and changing very fast, the levels of violence are high, and there is an environment of distrust in the eco system. These contacts are used as leverages to bring down the levels of violence under tolerance limits and commence the negotiations once a hostage case takes place. We established communication with local civilians, leaders of AOGs, and field commanders of SAAF, in spite of the taboo by our host nation to contact any Syrian nationals directly.

Multi-Pronged Approach. A hostage case had to be addressed simultaneously at all levels; the field level, mission level, diplomatic level, regional level, and at the UN Headquarters levels. I maintained continuous interaction with diplomats from TCCs, P-5 Countries, Arabic speaking countries especially Qatar and Saudi Arabia in Lebanon and Jordan. My preliminary knowledge of Arabic language came really handy in breaking the ice.

Negotiations Tips. Mutual respect for each other's view point is paramount. Staying calm, cool and collected helps in getting closer to a resolution. Complete knowledge of the demography, area familiarisation, and the incident is a pre-requisite. The negotiator should exhibit confidence, conviction, moral high ground and a positive body language, and one must not be dismissive when the other side explains their view point. The negotiator has to highlight mission's transparency and impartiality and make the other side understand that we are not aligned to any side. Patient hearing and genuine efforts to alleviate miseries of local citizens is likely to show genuineness of the peacekeeping mission. One has to build a rapport and show accessibility and credibility. Initially, one must start at a higher moral pedestal and begin to give concessions incrementally. Breakdown of complex situations to a number of achievable or doable parts show progress and get us closer to the resolution. A trustworthy interpreter is a must. One should also know when to pull out and have adjournments to take stock of the situation and also come out with worthwhile concessions approved by empowered authority. Patience is a virtue that helps in prolonged negotiations. Don't ever promise anything beyond one's pay check.

Handling of Post-Traumatic Stress Disorder (PTSD) Cases. Having been taken a hostage is a very traumatic experience and is likely to have negative effect on the personality of affected peacekeepers. The affected peacekeepers need to be kept under a close watch and such cases need a very delicate handling. Preferably, place of work of the affected personnel should be changed to a more sedentary desk job. Expert counselling should be provided and the individual motivated to take help ensuring that no stigma is attached. After the initial formalities, the persons released from the custody must be sent on long leave to spend quality time with their families.

Perception Management and Use of Social Media. As per the Syrian Government, our host nation, we were not allowed to interact and maintain contact with their army or the local people. All issues were to be addressed through a one window opportunity by flagging our concerns through the Syrian Senior Arab Delegate (SSAD), a Brigadier General deputed from the Syrian Army. However, with the fluid security situation in the field, it was important to maintain contacts with all actors in order to ensure that we remained on top of the situation and were not ever taken by surprise. It helped in apprising people what the UN peacekeeping stands for and to build a favourable public opinion and use leverages to get the hostages released. Periodic press releases in the social and vernacular media had to be given in order to clearly show our position on all burning issues.

Mission Capability Study and Capacity Building. To enhance staying power in disturbed areas, we brought in adequate mitigation measures. Better situational awareness including sampling of incidents, leadership redundancies, posting of political advisors, maintaining strict chain of command and control; movement control & protection measures like bullet proof vehicles & counter IED equipment and beefed up security set up helped in reducing the abduction cases. We hardened and improved our positions to be able to return the fire when attacked by the AOGs/Government backed militia groups. Liaison capabilities were doubled and our medical support was upgraded to ensure appropriate handling of the casualties during the Golden Hour Period.

Conclusion

An incident of hostages crisis is a traumatic experience for the affected persons and their families and a cause of concern for the organisation. As the Head of the Mission and Force Commander, I always felt that it was my moral duty to get my men and women released safely at the earliest possible opportunity. Some minor incidents were sorted out within hours right there by show of force or persuasion. The minds of abductors are also confused in the initial stages but by and by their stance becomes tougher. However, it is essential to remain patient and cool and think of ways and means to get around the abductors or tire them out and make them release the hostages without any bodily or mental harm to the peacekeepers. Instituting all possible measures as good practices to ensure that hostage taking is prevented is paramount. Gauging the tipping point when the abductors may start torturing or killing the hostages is a very fine judgement and all decisions to prevent reaching that stage must be taken in good time. Prevention is always better than the cure.

Closing Remarks

Major General PK Goswami, VSM (Retd)

At the outset, my compliments to all the speakers, General Jatley, General Singha, Colonel (Dr) Sharma and our anchor Amb Dinkar Srivastava; he not only deliberated on the issue but also moderated the complete discussion.

Dr Raghavan, in opening remarks, raised very concerned and thought provoking issues related to hostage taking of UN Peacekeepers. He highlighted the increasing number of intra-state conflicts and growing intensity of the violence in the UN mission areas leading to peacekeepers themselves often becoming the target. To counter this growing threat to the peacekeepers, there is, therefore, now more emphasis on force protection measures and robust rules of engagement.

Amb Dinkar Srivastava, provided larger overview of Hostage Crisis to include challenges and response strategy, and set the stage for the subsequent speakers. He brought out that the hostage situation arose in Sierra Leone because the mandate was not matched by resources. The deployment of UN peacekeepers over an extended area in small strength made it easier for the rebels to surround them and take hostage. Break-down of peace accord had transformed this peacekeeping into peace-enforcement operation and needed stepping up of force level.

Colonel (Dr) Sharma highlighted challenges for the UN during hostage crisis like complexity for resolving the crisis due to multiple stakeholders i.e. UN HQ, the DPO and DPPA, Force HQ in the mission area, peacekeepers; TCCs and their leaning towards warring parties. No 'one fit all' solution possible since every situation is different, thus needs different line of action. He deliberated that hostage taking situations have come to the centre-stage due to ever present threat of insurgencies or terrorism, tremendous loss of lives, and ever present media. The goals of hostage takers are generally to gain political, criminal, and/or social benefits through a coercive or forced situation. Negotiation is a discreet form of diplomacy but national policies range from 'No Negotiation' to the 'Track II Negotiation'. These may also take a form of 'Regular Negotiation' or a 'Negotiation in order to prepare for an Assault'. No negotiation is a policy followed by most Western countries and is often applied during a hostage crisis. All of these have a direct relevance to the UN Peacekeeping scenarios.

General Jatley and General Singha brought out individual experiences and reflection on their experiences at Sierra Leone and Golan Heights during hostage crisis, thus provided deep insight into the issues which confront UN peacekeeping even today. They exposed us to whole range of the issues that were involved during hostage crisis such as coordination with UN HQ, TCCs, local governments, and multiple rebel groups; complexity due to these for timely decision making to resolve, and, finally, after crisis on issues related to mandate, equipping, and use of force. To free the hostages from their captors has multiple challenges, thus analysis of the past hostage incidents is important to draw lessons for prevention and resolution of such crisis in future. Prevention is always better than cure.

Infact, since the tragic bombing of the UN HQ in Iraq in 2003, a concerted effort has been made across the UN system to improve and strengthen security arrangements. However, too often, security issues are perceived as primarily technical matters and are not prioritised as strategically and politically important. The increasingly volatile environments into which UN peace operations are deployed today and the demanding tasks being mandated require immediate and serious consideration of security issues. The 2008 'Report of the Independent Panel on Safety and Security of UN Personnel and Premises Worldwide', also known as the Brahimi Safety and Security Report, stated that the UN must recognise 'security as a strategic instrument for achieving substantive goals'.

Thus, it is time to take stock of the following issues for the safety and security of personnel in UN peace operations:

(a) Selection of the appropriate resources by the Security Council for the mandate it is trying to accomplish.

(b) Approval of adequate budgetary support by the General Assembly.

(c) TCCs and PCCs are timely enabled and incentivised on the issues of concern, as considered and recommended by The Special Committee on Peacekeeping Operations (C34).

(d) Secretariat is empowered to proactively plan and manage security issues.

(e) Full support to Mission leadership.

(f) Build confidence among all personnel serving in UN peace operations that the UN values their service and will effectively execute its responsibility of care.

It has clearly come out in today's discussions that to counter this growing threat to the peacekeepers, there is now more awareness and emphasis on force protection measures and robust rules of engagement. Even the mandates have become stronger allowing the peacekeepers to use force and any other means as necessary to ensure their safety.

To share the rich experiences of speakers with larger audience and cross fertilisation of ideas, we are compiling the speaker's addresses of each webinar into a monograph. I am glad to inform all that our first monograph on 'India and UN Peace Operations: Principles of UN Peacekeeping and Mandate' is already printed and available.

At the end, I express my gratitude to Dr Raghavan, DG, ICWA, for partnering with the USI for organising these webinars on the UN peacekeeping related issues. Of course, last but not the least, I also acknowledge the contribution of my dear friend Major General (Dr) AK Bardalai for his valuable support and assistance in conceptualisation and conduct of this series of webinars.

Our best wishes to all participants for joining us today and look forward to your continued support. Our forthcoming webinar is likely sometime in Aug/Sep 21 and theme will be either 'Effectiveness of Peace Operations' or 'Protection of Civilians in complex UN Peace Operations'.

Till we meet next - Stay safe, stay healthy.